SUPER SIMPLE

AUSTRALIAN ART

FUN AND EASY ART FROM AROUND THE WORLD

ALEX KUSKOWSKI

Super Sandcastle

An Imprint of Abdo Publishing
www.abdopublishing.com

Consulting Editor, Diane Craig,
M.A./Reading Specialist

VISIT US AT WWW.ABDOPUBLISHING.COM

Published by Abdo Publishing, a division of ABDO, PO Box 398166, Minneapolis, Minnesota 55439. Copyright © 2015 by Abdo Consulting Group, Inc. International copyrights reserved in all countries. No part of this book may be reproduced in any form without written permission from the publisher. Super SandCastle™ is a trademark and logo of Abdo Publishing.

Printed in the United States of America, North Mankato, Minnesota
062014
092014

THIS BOOK CONTAINS RECYCLED MATERIALS

Editor: Liz Salzmann
Content Developer: Nancy Tuminelly
Cover and Interior Design and Production: Mighty Media, Inc.
Photo Credits: Jen Schoeller, Shutterstock

The following manufacturers/names appearing in this book are trademarks: Scribbles®, Arm & Hammer®, General Mills Total®, Gold Metal®, Crystal Sugar®, Anderson's, Mod Podge®, Elmer's® Glue-All™, Roundy's®, ACE®, Sharpie®, UL®

Library of Congress Cataloging-in-Publication Data
Kuskowski, Alex., author.
 Super simple Australian art : fun and easy art from around the world / Alex Kuskowski ; consulting editor, Diane Craig, M.A., reading specialist.
     pages cm. -- (Super simple cultural art)
 Audience: Ages 5-10.
 ISBN 978-1-62403-278-3
1. Handicraft--Juvenile literature. 2. Art, Aboriginal Australian--Juvenile literature. 3. Australia--Civilization--Miscellanea--Juvenile literature. I. Craig, Diane, editor. II. Title. III. Series: Super simple cultural art.
 TT160.K8736 2015
 745.50994--dc23
                2013043461

Super SandCastle™ books are created by a team of professional educators, reading specialists, and content developers around five essential components—phonemic awareness, phonics, vocabulary, text comprehension, and fluency—to assist young readers as they develop reading skills and strategies and increase their general knowledge. All books are written, reviewed, and leveled for guided reading, early reading intervention, and Accelerated Reader® programs for use in shared, guided, and independent reading and writing activities to support a balanced approach to literacy instruction.

TO ADULT HELPERS

Children can have a lot of fun learning about different cultures through arts and crafts. Be sure to supervise them as they work on the projects in this book. Let the kids do as much as possible on their own. But be ready to step in and help if necessary. Also, kids may be using glue, paint, markers, and clay. Make sure they protect their clothes and work surfaces.

KEY SYMBOL

In this book you may see this **symbol**. Here is what it means.

HOT!
You will be working with something hot. Get help.

TABLE OF CONTENTS

KANGAROO

Kangaroos are found all over Australia. They are even on the Australian coat of arms.

COOL CULTURE

Get ready to go on a **cultural** art adventure! All around the world people make art. They use art to show different **traditions** and ideas. Learning about different cultures with art can be a lot of fun.

Australia is the only country that is also a continent. It has many nicknames! Australia is called "The Outback," "Down Under," and even "Oz."

Learn more about Australia! Try some of the art projects in this book. Get creative with culture using art.

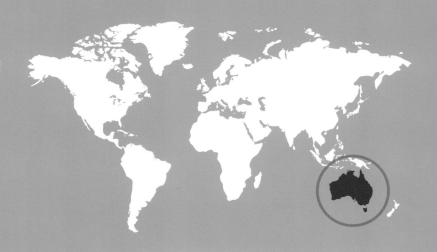

BEFORE YOU START

Remember to treat other people and **cultures** with respect. Respect their art, **jewelry**, and clothes too. These things can have special meaning to people.

There are a few rules for doing art projects:

▶ **PERMISSION**
Make sure to get **permission** to do a project. You might want to use things you find around the house. Ask first!

▶ **SAFETY**
Get help from an adult when using something hot or sharp. Never use a stove or oven by yourself.

ART IN AUSTRALIAN CULTURE

People in Australia create many beautiful things. Some are for everyday use. Others are for special occasions. The **designs** in Australian art often have special meanings.

 Aboriginal clapsticks are **traditional** instruments for many **Aboriginal** groups.

 The rainbow serpent is used in a lot of paintings. It stands for creation.

 The didgeridoo is a wind instrument. When you blow through one end, it makes a loud sound!

 The Koala is a **marsupial**. It is only found in the **rain forests** of Australia.

 Sheep are an important **resource** in Australia. There are over 70 million sheep living there!

 Ancient Australians made rock paintings. Some are thousands of years old.

 Aboriginal sign paintings are made up of **symbols**. They tell stories.

 Anzac biscuits are popular in Australia. They were used to feed soldiers during World War I.

WHAT YOU NEED

acrylic paint, puffy paint, paintbrush & foam brush

baking soda

beads

black cord

butter

card stock

cardboard wrapping paper tube

cereal box

cookie sheet & parchment paper

cotton swabs

corkboard

craft sticks

felt

flaked coconut

flour & sugar

fork & small bowl

glass jar

googly eyes

hot glue gun & glue sticks

key ring

large sewing needle

maple syrup

measuring cups and spoons

mixing bowls & mixing spoon

Mod Podge & craft glue

newspaper

oven mitts

paper plates

quick cooking oats

ruler

saucepan

scissors

Styrofoam egg & pom-poms

toothpicks

white pencil, marker & paint marker

wooden dowels & ribbon

wooden frame & flat rocks

ROCK ART FRAME

Make a timeless rock frame!

WHAT YOU NEED

- newspaper
- flat rocks
- red and yellow acrylic paint
- foam brush
- wooden frame
- yellow paint marker
- hot glue gun and glue sticks

DIRECTIONS

1. Cover your work area with newspaper. Paint all the rocks red. Let the paint dry. Paint another coat of red paint. Let it dry.

2. Paint the frame yellow. Let the paint dry.

3. Have an adult help you glue the rocks to the frame. Make sure to cover the wood. Let the glue dry.

4. Use the yellow paint marker to outline each rock. Make circles on the rocks.

SERPENT COASTER

Set your drink on a coiled snake!

WHAT YOU NEED

jar

marker

corkboard

black card stock

scissors

Mod Podge

white pencil

acrylic paint

paintbrush

foam brush

DIRECTIONS

1. Put the jar upside down on the corkboard. Trace around it. Trace it again on the card stock. Cut out the corkboard and card stock circles.

2. Glue the card stock circle to the corkboard circle. Let the glue dry.

3. Draw a snake on the card stock with the white pencil.

4. Paint in the snake in rainbow colors. Outline the snake with white paint. Paint the sides of the corkboard circle black. Let the paint dry.

5. Paint the top with two coats of Mod Podge. Let it dry between coats.

COME BACK BOOMERANG

The boomerang is used for hunting, sports, and games in Australia.

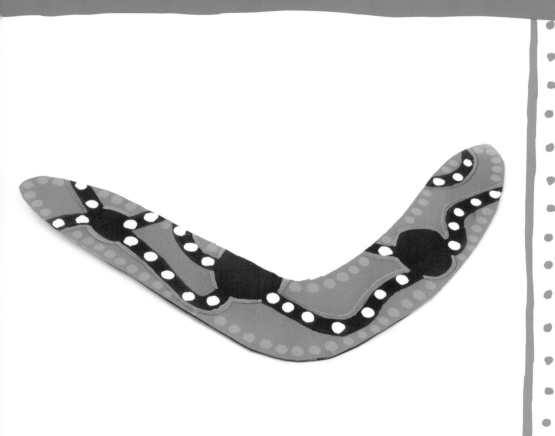

WHAT YOU NEED

cereal box

scissors

marker

red card stock

craft glue

acrylic paint

paintbrush

cotton swabs

DIRECTIONS

(1) Cut a large flat section from the cereal box. Draw a boomerang shape on the cardboard. Cut it out.

(2) Trace both sides of the boomerang on red card stock. Cut them both out. Glue one to each side of the cardboard boomerang.

(3) Paint trails on the boomerang in brown. In **Aboriginal** art, circles represent watering holes.

(4) Outline some of the shapes in blue. Use cotton swabs to add color. Add dots in orange and white.

QUICK TIP: **Research** to learn more Aboriginal art **symbols** you can use!

KANGAROO POUCH

Make a pencil holder!

WHAT YOU NEED

4 paper plates

scissors

newspaper

brown & black acrylic paint

foam brush

craft stick

glass jar,
4 inches (10 cm) tall

ruler

googly eyes

craft glue

paintbrush

hot glue gun and glue sticks

DIRECTIONS

1. Cut off the edges of all the paper plates.

2. Cover your work area with newspaper. Paint both sides of each plate, the craft stick, and the jar brown. Let the paint dry. Add a second coat if necessary.

3. Cut three ovals from one plate. Make two of them 2 inches (5 cm) long. Make the third 4 inches (10 cm) long. Cut the second paper plate in half.

PROJECT CONTINUES ON THE NEXT PAGE

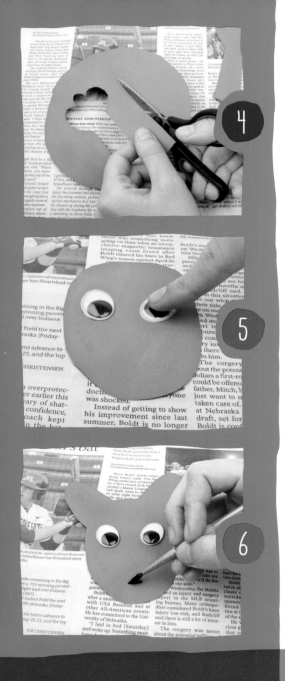

DIRECTIONS (CONTINUED)

(4) Cut two arms from the third paper plate. Cut two feet from the last paper plate.

(5) The large oval is the kangaroo's head. Glue the two googly eyes onto it.

(6) Glue the two small ovals to the larger oval for ears. Paint on a black nose. Let the paint dry.

DIRECTIONS (CONTINUED)

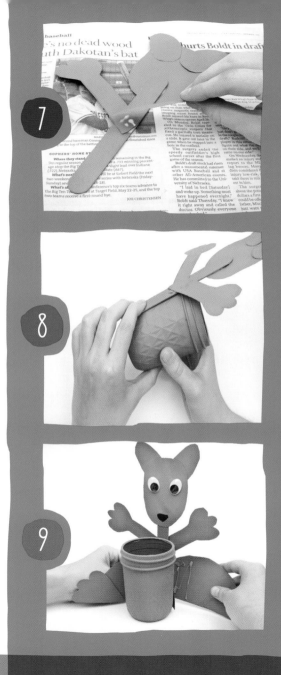

7. Glue the head to one end of the craft stick. Glue the arms to the back of the craft stick.

8. Have an adult help you hot glue the craft stick to the jar. Make sure the kangaroo's face is above the jar.

9. Lay the two half circles next to each other. Glue one foot to the left side of one half circle. Glue the other foot to the right side of the second half circle. These are the legs. Hot glue them to the back of the jar.

LOUD CLAPSTICKS

Clap along to the beat!

WHAT YOU NEED

newspaper

2 wooden dowels

acrylic paint

paintbrush

cotton swabs

green and purple ribbon

scissors

ruler

hot glue gun and glue sticks

DIRECTIONS

1 Cover your work area with newspaper. Paint the dowels orange. Let the paint dry.

2 Paint on bands in different colors. Add dots or animals. Let the paint dry.

3 Cut three purple ribbons 6 inches (15 cm) long. Cut three green ribbons the same size. Tie three of the ribbons together. Tie the knot in the middle of the ribbons.

4 Have an adult help you hot glue the knot to one end of a dowel. Tie the other three ribbons together. Glue the knot to the other dowel.

KOALA KEY CHAIN

Carry this cute koala with you!

WHAT YOU NEED

gray and white felt

marker

ruler

scissors

craft glue

googly eyes

large sewing needle

black cord

beads

key ring

DIRECTIONS

1. Draw an oval 3 inches (7.5 cm) across on gray felt. Draw two ears on either end of the oval. This is the koala's head. Cut it out.

2. Draw a large dot in the middle of the oval.

3. Draw two lines from the dot to the top of the oval. The lines should make a "v" shape.

PROJECT CONTINUES ON THE NEXT PAGE

DIRECTIONS (CONTINUED)

(4) Cut out the "v" shape.

(5) Glue the googly eyes on either side of the "v." Let the glue dry. Draw a mouth under the nose.

(6) Cut two small half circles out of white felt. Glue them onto the ears. Let the glue dry.

7   Cut a piece of cord 10 inches (25.5 cm) long. Thread it onto the needle.

DIRECTIONS (CONTINUED)

8. Bring the two sides of the "v" together. Push the needle through both corners from back to front. Pull until the cord is halfway through.

9. Bring the needle around to the back. Push it through the felt again. Pull it tight. Tie the cord in a knot.

10. Thread five beads onto each end of the cord. Tie the ends together. Cut off the extra cord. Add the key ring.

DOWN UNDER DIDGERIDOO

Play an instrument from the outback!

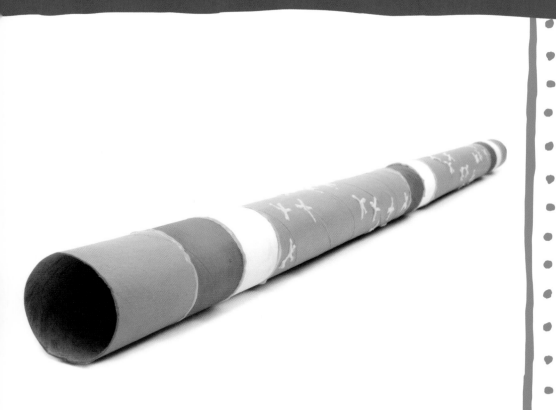

WHAT YOU NEED

newspaper

cardboard wrapping paper tube

acrylic paint

foam brush

puffy paint

26

DIRECTIONS

1. Cover your work area with newspaper.

2. Paint the cardboard tube blue. Let the paint dry. Paint another coat of blue paint. Let it dry.

3. Paint on three bands of red and white paint. Let the paint dry.

4. Use puffy paint to add animal tracks. Let the paint dry.

5. To play your didgeridoo, put your mouth against one end and hum.

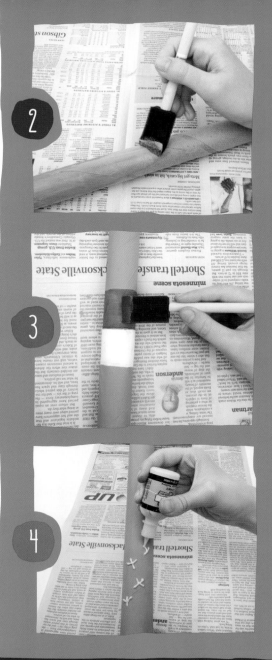

WOOLY SHEEP

Create a flock of your very own!

4 toothpicks

black acrylic paint

paintbrush

small black and white pom-poms

Styrofoam egg

hot glue gun and glue sticks

large black pom-pom

googly eyes

scissors

black felt

DIRECTIONS

1 Paint the toothpicks black. Let them dry.

2 Have an adult help you hot glue small white pom-poms to the Styrofoam egg. Cover the egg completely. Let it dry.

3 Hot glue the large black pom-pom to one end of the egg. Glue a small black pom-pom to the other end of the egg. Glue two googly eyes to the large black pom-pom.

4 Stick the toothpicks into the bottom of the egg. Put two toothpicks near the head. Put two toothpicks near the tail. Stick them in at an angle.

5 Cut two **petal** shapes out of felt. Glue them on the head for ears.

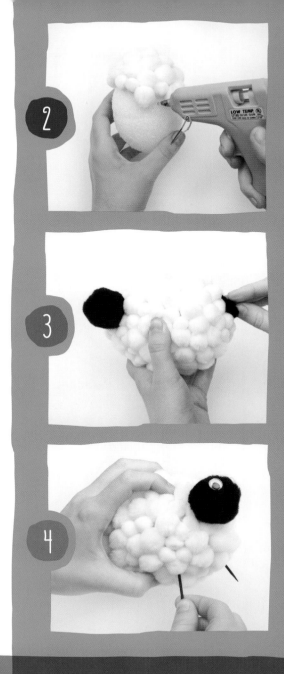

TASTY BISCUIT BITE

This favorite Australian treat is made for snacking!

WHAT YOU NEED

parchment paper
cookie sheet
measuring cups & spoons
1 cup quick cooking oats
1 cup flour
¾ cup flaked coconut
1 cup sugar
mixing bowl
mixing spoon
9 tablespoons butter
1 tablespoon maple syrup
saucepan
1 teaspoon baking soda
small bowl
fork
oven mitts

DIRECTIONS

1   Preheat the oven to 350. Put parchment paper on a cookie sheet.

(2) Put the oats, flour, coconut, and sugar in a mixing bowl. Stir and set aside.

3   Put the butter and maple syrup in a saucepan. Heat on low until the butter melts. Stir.

(4) Put the baking soda and 2 tablespoons hot water in a small bowl. Mix with a fork. Add the baking soda mixture to the butter mixture. Stir. Remove from heat.

(5) Add the butter mixture to the oats mixture. Mix together.

(6) Roll the **dough** into balls. Put them 2 inches (5 cm) apart on the cookie sheet. Bake 15 minutes.

GLOSSARY

Aboriginal – related to the people native to the Australian continent.

culture – the ideas, art, and other products of a particular group of people.

design – a decorative pattern or arrangement.

dough – a thick mixture of flour, water, and other ingredients used in baking.

jewelry – pretty things, such as rings and necklaces, that you wear for decoration.

marsupial – a mammal in which the female has a pouch in which the young develop.

permission – when a person in charge says it's okay to do something.

rain forest – a tropical wooded area that gets a lot of rain and has very tall trees.

research – to find out more about something.

resource – something that is usable or valuable.

petal – one of the thin, colored parts of a flower.

symbol – an object or picture that stands for or represents something.

tradition – a belief or practice passed through a family or group of people.